Contents

Published by Collins
An imprint of HarperCollins*Publishers*
The News Building, 1 London Bridge Street, London, SE1 9GF, UK

HarperCollins*Publishers*
Macken House, 39/40 Mayor Street Upper, Dublin 1, DO1 C9W8, Ireland

Browse the complete Collins catalogue at
www.collins.co.uk

British Library Cataloguing-in-Publication Data
A catalogue record for this publication is available from the British Library.

Compiled by: Fiona Macgregor
Publisher: Elaine Higgleton
Product manager: Letitia Luff
Commissioning editor: Rachel Houghton
Edited by: Hannah Hirst-Dunton
Editorial management: Oriel Square
Cover designer: Kevin Robbins
Cover illustrations: Jouve India Pvt. Ltd.
Additional text credit: p 3–11 Monica Hughes, p 12–21
Jessica Ellis, p 24–29 Anthony Robinson
Internal illustrations: p 3–11 Gustavo Mazili, p 12–21
Parwinder Singh, p 24–29 Gwyneth Williamson
Typesetter: Jouve India Pvt. Ltd.
Production controller: Lyndsey Rogers
Printed and bound in the UK using 100% Renewable
Electricity at Martins the Printers

Acknowledgements

With thanks to all the kindergarten staff and their schools around the world who have helped with the development of this course, by sharing insights and commenting on and testing sample materials:

Calcutta International School: Sharmila Majumdar, Mrs Pratima Nayar, Preeti Roychoudhury, Tinku Yadav, Lakshmi Khanna, Mousumi Guha, Radhika Dhanuka, Archana Tiwari, Urmita Das; Gateway College (Sri Lanka): Kousala Benedict; Hawar International School: Kareen Barakat, Shahla Mohammed, Jennah Hussain; Manthan International School: Shalini Reddy; Monterey Pre-Primary: Adina Oram; Prometheus School: Aneesha Sahni, Deepa Nanda; Pragyanam School: Monika Sachdev; Rosary Sisters High School: Samar Sabat, Sireen Freij, Hiba Mousa; Solitaire Global School: Devi Nimmagadda; United Charter Schools (UCS): Tabassum Murtaza and staff; Vietnam Australia International School: Holly Simpson

The publishers wish to thank the following for permission to reproduce photographs.

(t = top, c = centre, b = bottom, r = right, l = left)

p 22t fizkes/Shutterstock, p 22b Monkey Business Images/Shutterstock, p 23t FamVeld/Shutterstock, p 23b VIEWVEAR/Shutterstock, p 30t Pixel-Shot/Shutterstock

The picnic

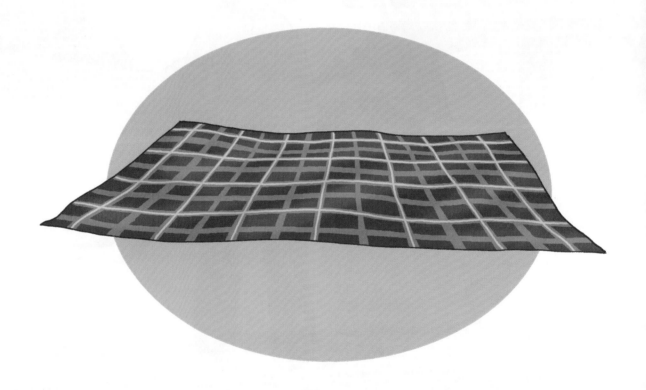

The rug

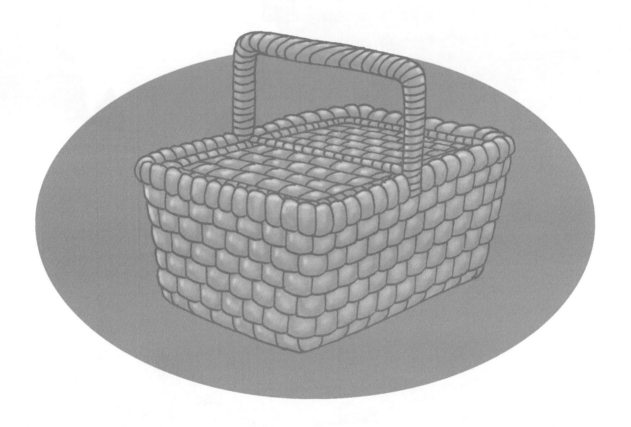

The basket

The cakes

The drinks

The wasps!

Finn feels better

Finn feels sad.

He and Mum go to his room.

Finn looks in the box.

He sees his things.

Finn can see his light.

He can see his art.

Finn sees his letters.

He sees his cool blanket.

Finn turns to Mum.

Wonderful water

We use water for drinking.

We use water for washing.

We use water to help plants grow.

We use water for transport.

Walking and walking

We like walking.

We like walking in the park.

We like walking on the beach.

We like walking in the woods.

We like walking home.

What is the time?

Wake-up time

 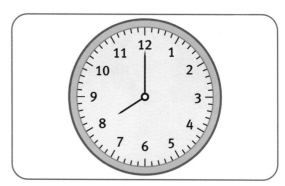

School time

Play time

Home time

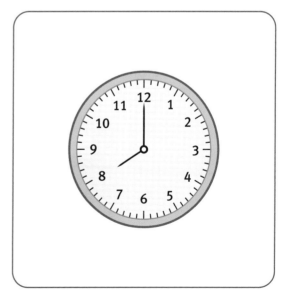

Bed time

Reading notes

Story	Sounds	Language structures
The picnic	'c', 'i', 'p', 'n'	Identifying the sight word *the*: *the* picnic, *the* food, *the* cake
Finn feels better	'f', 'd', 's', 'a'	Talking about feelings: *I feel...*
Wonderful water	'w', 'e', 'u'	Saying what we use water for: *We drink...*; *we use...*
Walking and walking	'e', 'p', 'b'	Talking about what we like: *We like...*
What is the time?	revision	Telling the time on the hour: *It is ... o'clock*

When you read these stories to your children at home, point out the new sound(s) in each story. Encourage your child to find the letter on the page. Then get them to say the sound, and the word, out loud.

Practise these language structures by asking questions. For example, ask: *How do you feel?* to elicit the response: *I feel happy/sad*, or ask: *What is the time?* to get the answer: *It is two o'clock*, or, *It is bed time.*